ANCIENT AND MEDIEVAL HISTORY

Guided Reading and Review Workbook

Needham, Massachusetts
Upper Saddle River, New Jersey
Glenview, Illinois

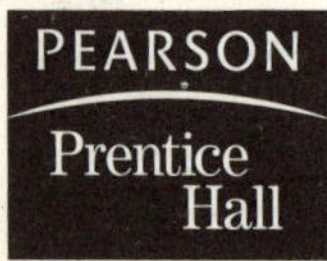

ISBN 0-13-067987-9

4 5 6 7 8 9 10   06 05 04 03

Success in social studies comes from doing three things well—reading, testing, and writing. The following pages present strategies to help you read for meaning, understand test questions, and write well.

Reading for Meaning

Do you have trouble remembering what you read? Here are some tips from experts that will improve your ability to recall and understand what you read:

BEFORE YOU READ

Preview the text to identify important information.
Like watching the coming attractions at a movie theater, previewing the text helps you know what to expect. Study the questions and strategies below to learn how to preview what you read.

Ask yourself these questions:	Use these strategies to find the answers:
• What is the text about?	Read the headings, subheadings, and captions. Study the photos, maps, tables, or graphs.
• What do I already know about the topic?	Read the questions at the end of the text to see if you can answer any of them.
• What is the purpose of the text?	Turn the headings into *who, what, when, where, why,* or *how* questions. This will help you decide if the text compares things, tells a chain of events, or explains causes and effects.

Organize information in a way that helps you see meaningful connections or relationships.

Taking notes as you read will improve your understanding. Use graphic organizers like the ones below to record the information you read. Study these descriptions and examples to learn how to create each type of organizer.

Sequencing

A **flowchart** helps you see how one event led to another. It can also display the steps in a process.

Use a flowchart if the text—
• tells about a chain of events.
• explains a method of doing something.

TIP▶ List the events or steps in order.

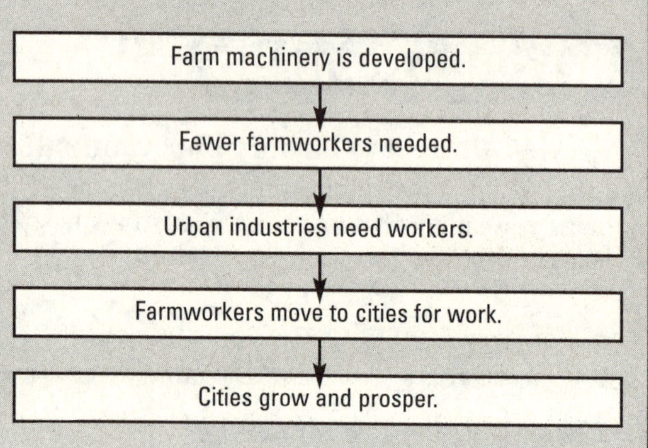

Comparing and Contrasting

A **Venn diagram** displays similarities and differences.

Use a Venn diagram if the text—
• compares and contrasts two individuals, groups, places, things, or events.

TIP▶ Label the outside section of each circle and list differences.
Label the shared section and list similarities.

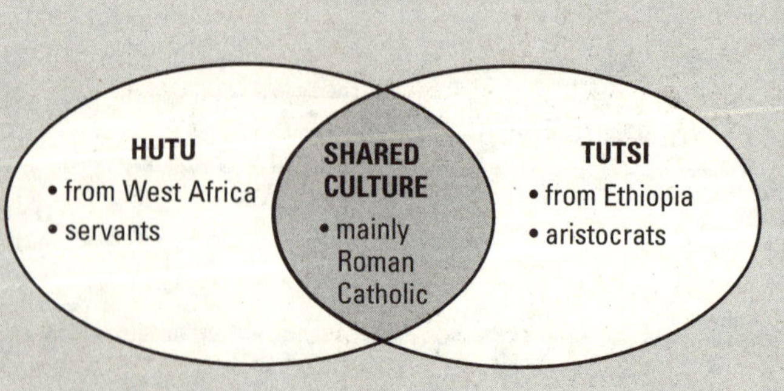

Categorizing Information

A **chart** organizes information in categories.

Use a chart if the text—
- lists similar facts about several places or things.
- presents characteristics of different groups.

TIP▶ Write an appropriate heading for each column in the chart to identify its category.

COUNTRY	FORM OF GOVERNMENT	ECONOMY
Cuba	communist dictatorship	command economy
Puerto Rico	democracy	free enterprise system

Identifying Main Ideas and Details

A **concept web** helps you understand relationships among ideas.

Use a concept web if the text—
- provides examples to support a main idea.
- links several ideas to a main topic.

TIP▶ Write the main idea in the largest circle. Write details in smaller circles and draw lines to show relationships.

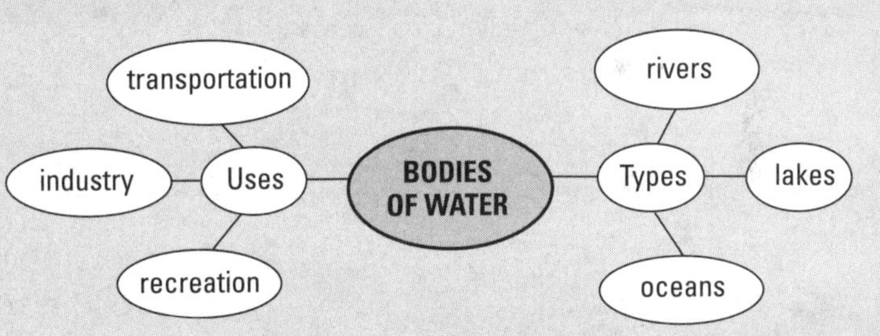

An **outline** provides an overview, or a kind of
blueprint for reading.

Use an outline to organize ideas—
- according to their importance.
- according to the order in which they are presented.

TIP▶ Use Roman numerals for main ideas, capital
letters for secondary ideas, and Arabic numerals
for supporting details.

> **I. Differences Between the North and the South**
>   **A.** Views on slavery
>   **1.** Northern abolitionists
>   **2.** Southern slave owners
>   **B.** Economies
>   **1.** Northern manufacturing
>   **2.** Southern agriculture

Identifying Cause and Effect

A **cause-and-effect** diagram shows the relationship
between what happened (effect) and the reason
why it happened (cause).

Use a cause-and-effect chart if the text—
- lists one or more causes for an event.
- lists one or more results of an event.

TIP▶ Label causes and effects. Draw arrows to
indicate how ideas are related.

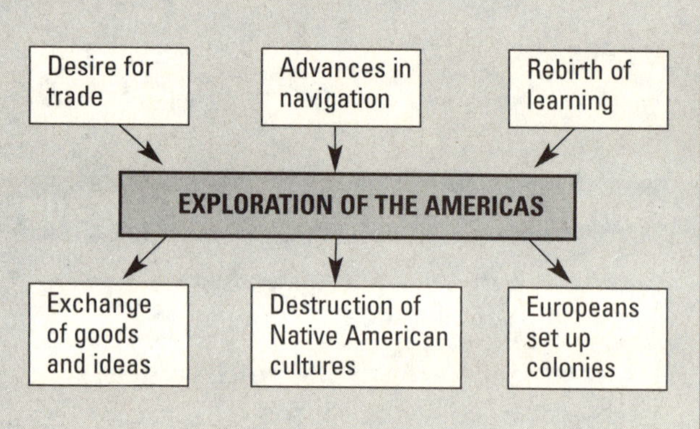

AFTER YOU READ

Test yourself to find out what you learned from reading the text.

Go back to the questions you asked yourself before you read the text. You
should be able to give more complete answers to these questions:
- What is the text about?
- What is the purpose of the text?

You should also be able to make connections between the new information
you learned from the text and what you already knew about the topic.

Study your graphic organizer. Use this information as the *answers*. Make up a
meaningful *question* about each piece of information.

Taking Tests

Do you panic at the thought of taking a standardized test? Here are some tips that most test developers recommend to help you achieve good scores.

MULTIPLE-CHOICE QUESTIONS

Read each part of a multiple-choice question to make sure you understand what is being asked.

Many tests are made up of multiple-choice questions. Some multiple-choice items are **direct questions.** They are complete sentences followed by possible answers, called distractors.

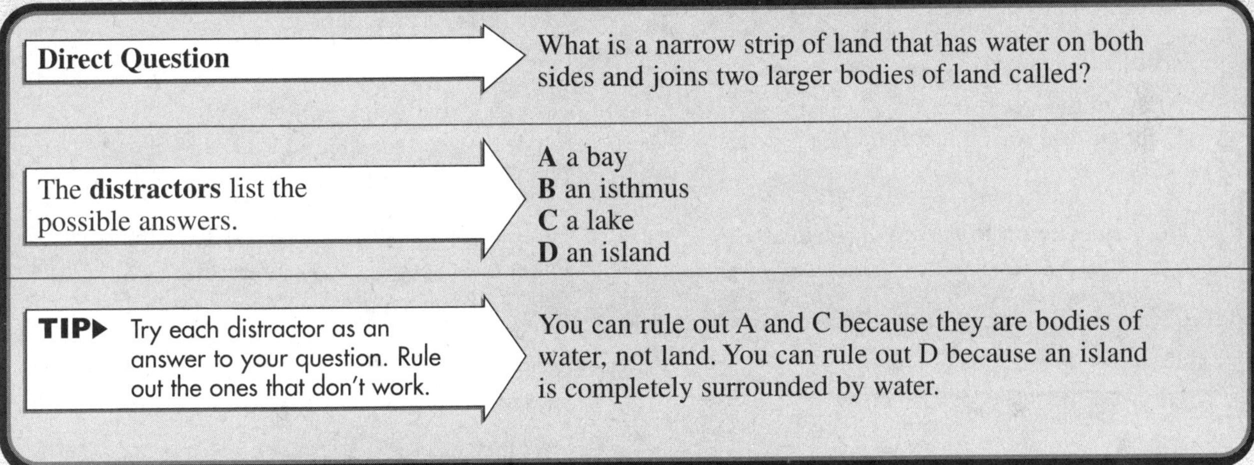

Other multiple-choice questions are **incomplete sentences** that you are to finish. They are followed by possible answers.

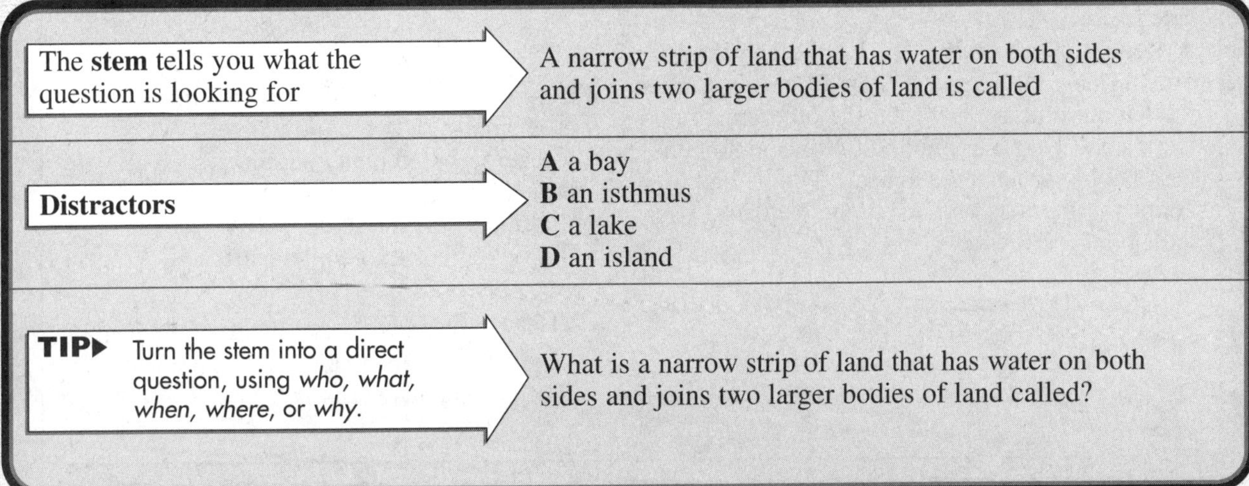

Identify the type of question you are being asked.

Social studies tests often ask questions that involve reading comprehension. Other questions may require you to gather or interpret information from a map, graph, or chart. The following strategies will help you answer different kinds of questions.

Reading Comprehension Questions

What to do:

1. Determine the content and organization of the selection.

2. Analyze the questions.
Do they ask you to *recall facts?*

Do they ask you to *make judgments?*

3. Read the selection.

4. Answer the questions.

How to do it:

Read the **title.** Skim the selection. Look for key words that indicate time, cause-and-effect, or comparison.

Look for **key words** in the stem:
<u>According to</u> the selection . . .
The selection <u>states</u> that . . .

The <u>main idea</u> of the selection is . . .
The author <u>would likely</u> agree that . . .

Read quickly. Keep the questions in mind.

Try out each distractor and choose the best answer. Refer back to the selection if necessary.

Example:

A Region of Diversity The Khmer empire was one of many kingdoms in Southeast Asia. Unlike the Khmer empire, however, the other kingdoms were small because Southeast Asia's mountains kept people protected and apart. People had little contact with those who lived outside their own valley.

Why were most kingdoms in Southeast Asia small?
A disease killed many people
B lack of food
C climate was too hot
D mountains kept people apart

TIP▶ The key word <u>because</u> tells why the kingdoms were small.
(The correct answer is D.)

(continued)

Map Questions

What to do:

1. Determine what kind of information is presented on the map.

How to do it:

Read the map **title.** It will indicate the purpose of the map.
Study the **map key.** It will explain the symbols used on the map.
Look at the **scale.** It will help you calculate distance between places on the map.

2. Read the question. Determine which component on the map will help you find the answer.

Look for **key words** in the stem.
About <u>how far</u> . . . [use the scale]
<u>What crops</u> were grown in . . . [use the map key]

3. Look at the map and answer the question in your own words.

Do not read the distractors yet.

4. Choose the best answer.

Decide which distractor agrees with the answer you determined from the map.

Eastern Europe: Language Groups

In which of these countries are Thraco-Illyrian languages spoken?

A Romania
B Albania
C Hungary
D Lithuania

TIP▶ Read the labels and the key to understand the map.
(The correct answer is B.)

What to do:

1. Determine the purpose of the graph.

2. Determine what information on the graph will help you find the answer.

3. Choose the best answer.

How to do it:

Read the graph **title.** It indicates what the graph represents.

Read the **labels** on the graph or on the key. They tell the units of measurement used by the graph.

Decide which distractor agrees with the answer you determined from the graph.

Example

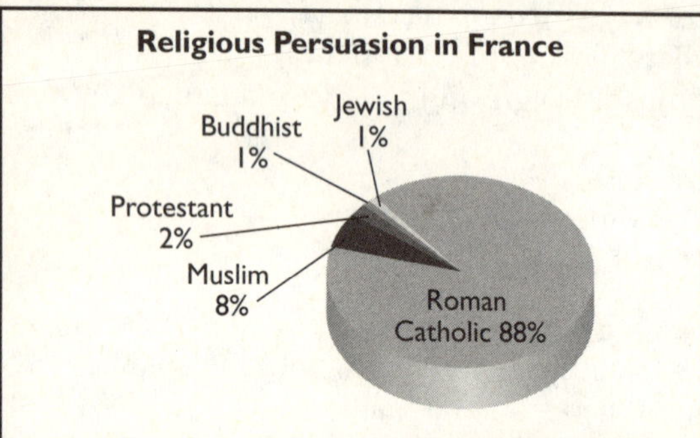

A **Circle graph** shows the relationship of parts to the whole in terms of percentages.

After Roman Catholics, the next largest religious population in France is
A Buddhist   **C** Jewish
B Protestant   **D** Muslim

TIP▶ Compare the percentages listed in the labels. (The correct answer is D.)

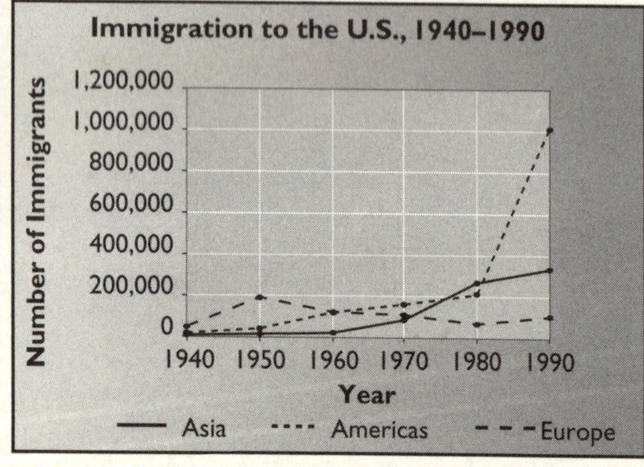

A **line graph** shows a pattern or change over time by the direction of the line.

Between 1980 and 1990, immigration to the U.S. from the Americas
A decreased a little   **C** stayed about the same
B increased greatly   **D** increased a little

TIP▶ Compare the vertical distance between the two correct points on the line graph. (The correct answer is B.)

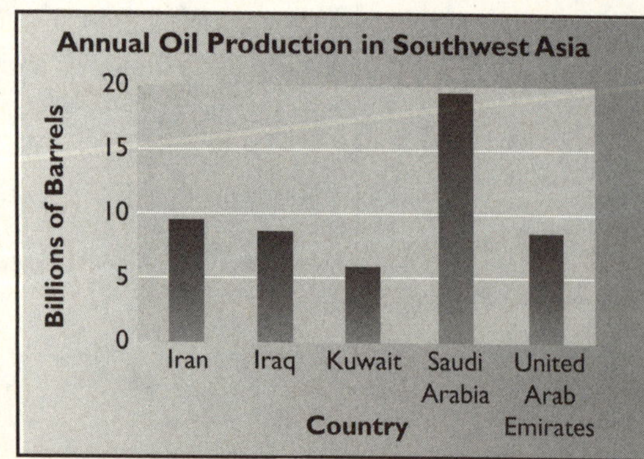

A **bar graph** compares differences in quantity by showing bars of different lengths.

Saudi Arabia produces about how many more billion of barrels of oil a year than Iran?
A 5 million   **C** 15 million
B 10 million   **D** 20 million

TIP▶ Compare the heights of the bars to find the difference. (The correct answer is B.)

Writing for Social Studies

When you face a writing assignment, do you think, "How will I ever get through this?" Here are some tips to guide you through any writing project from start to finish.

THE WRITING PROCESS

Follow each step of the writing process to communicate effectively.

Step 1. Prewrite

- Establish the purpose.
- Define the topic.
- Determine the audience.
- Gather details.

Step 2. Draft

- Organize information logically in an outline or graphic organizer.
- Write an introduction, body, and conclusion.
- State main ideas clearly.
- Include relevant details to support your ideas.

Step 3. Revise

- Edit for clarity of ideas and elaboration.

Step 4. Proofread

- Correct any errors in spelling, grammar, and punctuation.

Step 5. Publish and Present

- Copy text neatly by hand, or use a typewriter or word processor.
- Illustrate as needed.
- Create a cover, if appropriate.

Identify the purpose for your writing.

Each type of writing assignment has a specific purpose, and each purpose needs a different plan for development. The following descriptions and examples will help you identify the three purposes for social studies writing. The lists of steps will help you plan your writing.

Writing to Inform

Purpose: to present facts or ideas

Example

During the 1960s, research indicated the dangers of the insecticide DDT. It killed insects but also had long-term effects. When birds and fish ate poisoned insects, DDT built up in their fatty tissue. The poison also showed up in human beings who ate birds and fish contaminated by DDT.

TIP▶ Look for these **key terms** in the assignment: explain, describe, report, narrate

How to get started:
- Determine the topic you will write about.
- Write a topic sentence that tells the main idea.
- List all the ideas you can think of that are related to the topic.
- Arrange the ideas in logical order.

Writing to Persuade

Purpose: to influence someone

Example

Teaching computer skills in the classroom uses time that could be spent teaching students how to think for themselves or how to interact with others. Students who can reason well, express themselves clearly, and get along with other people will be better prepared for life than those who can use a computer.

TIP▶ Look for these **key terms** in the assignment: convince, argue, request

How to get started:
- Make sure you understand the problem or issue clearly.
- Determine your position.
- List evidence to support your arguments.
- Predict opposing views.
- List evidence you can use to overcome the opposing arguments.

Writing to Provide Historical Interpretations

Purpose: to present the perspective of someone in a different era

Example

The crossing took a week, but the steamship voyage was hard. We were cramped in steerage with hundreds of others. At last we saw the huge statue of the lady with the torch. In the reception center, my mother held my hand while the doctor examined me. Then, my father showed our papers to the official, and we collected our bags. I was scared as we headed off to find a home in our new country.

TIP▶ Look for these **key terms** in the assignment: go back in time, create, suppose that, if you were

How to get started:
- Study the events or issues of the time period you will write about.
- Consider how these events or issues might have affected different people at the time.
- Choose a person whose views you would like to present.
- Identify the thoughts and feelings this person might have experienced.

RESEARCH FOR WRITING

Follow each step of the writing process to communicate effectively.

After you have identified the purpose for your writing, you may need to do research. The following steps will help you plan, gather, organize, and present information.

Step 1. Ask Questions

Ask yourself questions to help guide your research.	What do I already know about the topic? What do I want to find out about the topic?

Step 2. Acquire Information

Locate and use appropriate sources of information about the topic.	Library Internet search Interviews
Take notes.	Follow accepted format for listing sources.

Step 3. Analyze Information

Evaluate the information you find.	Is it relevant to the topic? Is it up-to-date? Is it accurate? Is the writer an authority on the topic? Is there any bias?

Step 4. Use Information

Answer your research questions with the information you have found. (You may find that you need to do more research.)	Do I have all the information I need?
Organize your information into the main points you want to make. Identify supporting details.	Arrange ideas in outline form or in a graphic organizer.

Step 5. Communicate What You've Learned

Review the purpose for your writing and choose an appropriate way to present the information.	**Purpose** **Presentation**

Purpose	Presentation
inform	formal paper, documentary, multimedia
persuade	essay, letter to the editor, speech
interpret	journal, newspaper account, drama

Draft and revise your writing, and then evaluate it.	Use a rubric for self-evaluation.

EVALUATING YOUR WRITING

Use the following rubric to help you evaluate your writing.

	Excellent	Good	Acceptable	Unacceptable
Purpose	Achieves purpose—to inform, persuade, or provide historical interpretation—very well	Informs, persuades, or provides historical interpretation reasonably well	Reader cannot easily tell if the purpose is to inform, persuade, or provide historical interpretation	Lacks purpose
Organization	Develops ideas in a very clear and logical way	Presents ideas in a reasonably well-organized way	Reader has difficulty following the organization	Lacks organization
Elaboration	Explains all ideas with facts and details	Explains most ideas with facts and details	Includes some supporting facts and details	Lacks supporting details
Use of Language	Uses excellent vocabulary and sentence structure with no errors in spelling, grammar, or punctuation	Uses good vocabulary and sentence structure with very few errors in spelling, grammar, or punctuation	Includes some errors in grammar, punctuation, and spelling	Includes many errors in grammar, punctuation, and spelling

CHAPTER 1
The World of Geography

The Five Themes of Geography

A. As You Read

Directions: As you read Section 1, answer the following questions in the space provided.

1. What two questions do geographers try to answer while studying different places?

____

2. How do the five themes—location, place, human-environment interaction, movement, and regions—help geographers when they study the Earth?

____

3. What are two different ways to describe a location?

____

4. Which way of describing location is being used when a geographer explains that a river is 250 miles north of San Antonio?

____

5. Why is the study of movement useful to geographers?

____

B. Reviewing Key Terms

Directions: Complete each sentence by writing the correct term in the blank provided.

6. The study of the Earth and its people is called _______________________ .

7. An invisible line that forms an east–west circle around the Earth is called both a(n)

_______________________ and line of _______________________ .

8. An imaginary line that circles the Earth from north to south is called both a(n)

_______________________ and line of _______________________ .

9. Geographers measure locations east or west of the _______________________ , which is numbered 0 degrees.

10. The parallel in the middle of the globe is called the _______________________ .

11. A unit used by geographers to measure location on maps is called a(n)

_______________________ .

12. A region of flat land is called a _______________________ .

GUIDED READING AND REVIEW

The Geographer's Tools

A. As You Read

Directions: As you read Section 2, fill in the table below. Under each main idea, write two supporting statements.

Main Idea A
A long time ago, few people knew anything about the land and water beyond their homes or neighborhoods.

1. ____

____

2. ____

____

Main Idea B
Globes are an accurate way of presenting information about the Earth, but flat maps are generally a better way of mapping the Earth.

3. ____

____

4. ____

____

B. Reviewing Key Terms

Directions: Complete each sentence by writing the correct term in the blank provided.

5. When a landmass looks larger on a map than it does on the globe, that change in shape is called ___________________ .

6. The symbols that appear on a map are explained in the ___________________ , or legend.

7. A round ball called a(n) ___________________ shows the Earth in a smaller size, or ___________________ .

8. Geographers call a Mercator ___________________ a conformal map.

9. A map usually has a compass ___________________ showing the ___________________ , which are north, south, east, and west.

CHAPTER 2
Earth's
Physical
Geography

Our Planet, the Earth

A. As You Read

Directions: As you read Section 1, answer the following questions in the space provided.

1. Why is our galaxy called the Milky Way?

____

____

2. Why are days longer than nights at certain times of the year?

____

____

3. When does the summer solstice occur in the Northern Hemisphere?

____

____

4. Why is it almost always hot in the area called the tropics?

____

____

B. Reviewing Key Terms

Directions: Complete each sentence by writing the correct term in the blank provided.

5. The imaginary line running through the Earth between the North and the South poles

   is called the _______________________ .

6. The polar zones are also called the _______________________ latitudes.

7. Temperate zones, or _______________________ latitudes, have different seasons throughout
   the year.

8. The oval-shaped path that the Earth takes around the sun is called a(n)

   _______________________ .

9. As the Earth travels around the sun, it spins on its axis, making a full
   _______________________ about every 24 hours.

10. Each year, the Earth makes one _______________________ around the sun.

11. It is almost always hot in the tropics, or _______________________ latitudes.

GUIDED READING AND REVIEW

Land, Air, and Water

A. As You Read

Directions: As you read Section 2, fill in the table below with information about continents. Under each main idea, write two supporting statements.

Main Idea A
Geographers theorize that millions of years ago, there was only one giant landmass, called Pangaea, on the Earth.

1. ____

____

2. ____

____

Main Idea B
The continents are parts of plates in the Earth's crust that over time move and shift in different directions.

3. ____

____

4. ____

____

B. Reviewing Key Terms

Directions: Complete each sentence by writing the correct term in the blank provided.

5. A landform that is wide at the bottom and rises more than 2,000 feet (610 m) above sea level to a narrow peak is called a(n) _______________ . A landform that is lower with a rounded top is called a(n) _______________ .

6. A flat area or an area with gently rolling land is called a(n) _______________ .

7. A flat area that rises above the surrounding land is called a(n) _______________ .

8. A shape or type of land, such as a mountain or hill, is called a(n) _______________ .

9. Each huge piece of the Earth's crust is called a(n) _______________ .

10. The idea that the Earth's outer skin is broken into huge plates is the theory of _______________ .

CHAPTER 2
Earth's Physical Geography

Climate and What Influences It

A. As You Read

Directions: As you read Section 3, complete the statements below.

1. The climate of an area is the average _______________________ over many years.

2. Fast moving rivers in the ocean, called _______________________ , are caused by the Earth's rotation.

3. In the summertime, a town near a lake or an ocean will usually be _______________________ than an area farther away from the water.

4. As well as making climates milder, wind and water can cause _______________________ to develop.

5. Violent wind and rain storms that form over the tropics in the Atlantic Ocean are called

_______________________ . Similar storms that form over the Pacific Ocean are called

_______________________ .

6. Tornadoes are twisting and swirling funnels of _______________________ that can sometimes reach 200 miles per hour.

B. Reviewing Key Terms

Directions: In the blanks provided, write the definitions for the following key terms.

7. weather

____

____

8. temperature

____

____

9. precipitation

____

____

10. climate

____

____

GUIDED READING AND REVIEW

How Climate Affects Vegetation

CHAPTER 2
Earth's
Physical
Geography

A. As You Read

Directions: As you read Section 4, fill in the table below with details about tropical, moderate, and polar climates.

Vegetation and Climate

	Tropical Climate	Moderate Climate	Polar Climate
Location	1.	2.	3.
Vegetation	4.	5.	6.
Seasons	7.	8.	9.

B. Reviewing Key Terms

Directions: In the blanks provided, write the definitions for the following key terms.

10. vegetation

____

____

11. canopy

____

____

12. tundra

____

____

13. vertical climate

____

____

CHAPTER 3
Earth's Human
Geography

Where Do People Live?

A. As You Read

Directions: As you read Section 1, answer the following questions in the space provided.

1. What three things do demographers examine to understand population distribution?

____

2. About what percentage of the world's population live in Asia, Europe, and North America?

____

3. What areas are difficult for people to live in?

____

4. Along what types of geographic features did most major civilizations begin?

____

5. Why did few people settle in the Great Plains of the United States at first?

____

6. How do some people manage to live comfortably in extremely hot or cold climates?

____

B. Reviewing Key Terms

Directions: In the blanks provided below, write the definitions for the following key terms.

7. population

____

____

8. population distribution

____

____

9. demographer

____

____

10. population density

____

GUIDED READING AND REVIEW

A Growing Population

A. As You Read

Directions: As you read Section 2, fill in the table below with information about population growth.

Causes and Effects of Population Growth

Cause	Effect
A hundred years ago in the United States, the death rate was higher, food supplies were scarce, and many died of diseases.	1.
The birthrate has increased quickly and the death rate has slowed.	2.
New medicines and types of surgery treat health problems and fight diseases.	3.
4.	Some nations in Southwest Asia face shortages of fresh water and energy.
5.	Forests in India and Pakistan are disappearing, affecting the supply of clean air.

B. Reviewing Key Terms

Directions: Complete each sentence by writing the correct term in the blank.

6. The average number of years a woman in the United States is projected to live, also

    known as her _________________ , is 80 years.

7. The changes made in farming methods during the 1950s are called

    the _________________ .

8. The number of live births per 1,000 people each year is called the _________________ .

9. When a country's birthrate is higher than its _________________ , its population is
    growing.

CHAPTER 3
Earth's Human Geography

Why People Migrate

A. As You Read

Directions: As you read Section 3, fill in the table below with information about migration. Under each main idea, write two supporting statements.

<table>
<tr><td colspan="2" align="center">Main Idea A</td></tr>
<tr><td colspan="2" align="center">The "push-pull" theory explains many immigration trends in history.</td></tr>
<tr><td>I.</td><td></td></tr>
<tr><td>2.</td><td></td></tr>
<tr><td colspan="2" align="center">Main Idea B</td></tr>
<tr><td colspan="2" align="center">Although many people leave their own countries for others, migration can occur within a country, too.</td></tr>
<tr><td>3.</td><td></td></tr>
<tr><td>4.</td><td></td></tr>
</table>

B. Reviewing Key Terms

Directions: Complete each sentence by writing the correct term in the blank provided.

5. The idea that certain reasons, often economic, cause people to move from one place to another is known as the _______________________ .

6. A person who _______________________ , or moves from one place to another, is called a(n) _______________________ .

7. A city or town is sometimes called a(n) _______________________ area. A less populated village is sometimes called a(n) _______________________ area.

8. Many people move from small towns to cities. This movement is called _______________________ .

1

What Is Culture?

A. As You Read

Directions: As you read Section 1, complete the statements below.

1. Geographers use levels of technology to see how _______________ a culture is.

2. In Bali, Indonesia, people carved _______________ into mountains to create farmland.

3. Before the Agricultural Revolution, people relied upon _______________ for most of their food.

4. When people learned how to make and use fire, some people began living in areas with _______________ climates.

5. A culture becomes a civilization when its people create a system of _______________ to save knowledge and pass it on to others.

B. Reviewing Key Terms

Directions: In the blanks provided, write the definitions for the following key terms.

6. culture

____

____

7. cultural trait

____

____

8. technology

____

____

9. cultural landscape

____

____

10. agriculture

____

____

CHAPTER 4
Cultures of the World

Social Groups, Language, and Religion

A. As You Read

Directions: As you read Section 2, fill in the table below with information about cultures.
Under each main idea, write two supporting statements.

Main Idea A
Each culture has its own social structure, or system of small groups within larger groups.
1. ____
2. ____

Main Idea B
Every culture is based on language.
3. ____
4. ____

B. Reviewing Key Terms

Directions: In the blanks provided, write the definitions for the following key terms.

5. social structure

____

6. nuclear family

____

7. extended family

____

8. ethics

____

Economic and Political Systems

A. As You Read

Directions: As you read Section 3, fill in the table below with details about the three
basic economic systems.

Facts About Economic Systems

	Capitalism	Socialism	Communism
Who owns businesses?	1.	2.	3.
Who decides how much to pay workers and how to use profits?	4.	5.	6.

B. Reviewing Key Terms

Directions: Complete each sentence by writing the correct term(s) in the blank(s) provided.

7. When a king or a queen rules a government, the system is called a(n)

   _____________________ .

8. A system that sets up and enforces the laws of a society is called a(n)

   _____________________ .

9. A person who receives a good or service is called a(n) _____________________ .

10. In early governments, people lived in small groups and ran the day-to-day affairs of those

    groups. This form of government is called a(n) _____________________ .

11. The three basic economic systems are called _____________________ ,

    _____________________ , and _____________________ .

12. A person who has almost total control over a country is called a(n)

    _____________________ .

13. When citizens elect representatives to run a country, it is called a(n)

    _____________________ .

CHAPTER 4
**Cultures of
the World**

Cultural Change

A. As You Read

Directions: As you read Section 4, answer the following questions in the space provided.

1. What are some things that can affect culture?

____

____

2. How does the story about jeans explain cultural diffusion?

____

____

3. What is an example of acculturation in sports today?

____

____

4. How has new technology sped up the process of cultural change?

____

____

5. Why do some people refer to the Earth as a "global village"?

____

____

6. How have cultures changed in relation to the environment?

____

____

B. Reviewing Key Terms

Directions: In the blanks provided, write the definitions for the following key terms.

7. cultural diffusion

____

____

8. acculturation

____

____

GUIDED READING AND REVIEW

What Are Natural Resources?

A. As You Read

Directions: As you read Section 1, fill in the chart below with information about natural resources.

Original Resource	Type of Resource	Possible Uses
Tree	1.	2.
Corn	3.	4.
Water	5.	6.
Natural Gas	7.	8.

B. Reviewing Key Terms

Directions: In the blanks provided, write the definitions for the following key terms.

9. natural resource

____

____

10. raw material

____

____

11. recyclable resource

____

____

12. renewable resource

____

____

13. nonrenewable resource

____

____

14. fossil fuel

____

____

CHAPTER 5
Earth's Natural Resources

How People Use the Land

A. As You Read

Directions: As you read Section 2, answer the following questions in the space provided.

1. In which stage of economic activity do people turn raw materials into things they use?

____

2. What happened during the Industrial Revolution?

____

3. What types of things can stop the movement of goods and services from one country to another?

____

4. What are some challenges that developing nations face?

____

B. Reviewing Key Terms

Directions: Complete each sentence by writing the correct term in the blank provided.

5. Farming done on large farms owned by companies instead of single families is called

_______________________ .

6. The governments of developed countries often give loans, or _______________________ , to the governments of developing nations.

7. When farmers grow only enough food to feed their own families, they practice

_______________________ .

8. A commercial farm that employs many workers but is owned by only a few people

is called a(n) _______________________ .

9. A country that has few industries is called a(n) _______________________ nation, whereas a country with many industries is called a(n) _______________________ nation.

10. The process of changing a raw material into a finished product is known as

_______________________ .

GUIDED READING AND REVIEW

People's Effect on the Environment

A. As You Read

Directions: As you read Section 3, fill in the table below with information about people and the environment. Under each main idea, write two supporting statements.

Main Idea A
Living things are tied to their ecosystems, and certain changes can destroy those ecosystems.

I. ____

____

2. ____

____

Main Idea B
Many countries and organizations are making efforts to reduce the use of things that are harmful to the environment.

3. ____

____

4. ____

____

B. Reviewing Key Terms

Directions: Complete each sentence by writing the correct term in the blank provided.

5. One way to prevent an endangered species from dying out is to defend the environment it lives in, or its ___________________ .

6. A layer of gas in the upper atmosphere called the ___________________ blocks most of the harmful ultraviolet rays from the sun.

7. Most American city governments encourage people to ___________________ many used materials such as newspapers, bottles, and cans.

8. When chemicals combine with water vapor in the air, they form ___________________ .

9. The release of greenhouse gases in the air may be the cause of ___________________ .

10. The Sahara and the Amazon River valley are examples of ___________________ .

11. The process of cutting down forests is called ___________________ .

CHAPTER 1
**The Beginnings
of Human
Society**

Geography and History

A. As You Read

Directions: As you read Section 1, answer the following questions in the space provided.

1. What did scientists learn from the Iceman's copper ax?

____

____

2. What other clues did scientists use to learn about the Iceman's life?

____

3. In what parts of the world did people first develop a system of writing?

____

4. Even though oral traditions might contain stories that are not historically accurate, what can they tell us about the past?

____

5. Why does the study of the geography of Egypt help us to better understand Egyptian civilization?

____

____

B. Reviewing Key Terms

Directions: Complete each sentence by writing the correct term in the blank provided.

6. The period of time in the past before writing was invented is known as

_______________________ .

7. Scientists who examine objects to learn about past people and cultures are known as

_______________________ .

8. The written records studied by historians often began as _______________________ , or stories passed down by word of mouth.

9. The recorded events of people are known as _______________________ .

GUIDED READING AND REVIEW

Prehistory

A. As You Read

Directions: As you read Section 2, fill in the table below with information about early humans. Under each main idea, write two supporting details.

Main Idea A
The ability to make crude stone tools was an important step in the development of human civilization.

1. ____

____

____

2. ____

____

____

Main Idea B
The growing of crops was one of the most important developments in the history of human civilization.

3. ____

____

____

4. ____

____

____

B. Reviewing Key Terms

Directions: Complete each sentence by writing the correct term in the blank provided.

5. People who have no single, settled home and who travel from place to place in search

of food are called _________________ .

6. Plants grow well in _________________ soil, which contains the substances they need
to grow.

7. During the New Stone Age, humans learned to tame, or _________________ ,
wild animals.

CHAPTER 1
**The Beginnings
of Human
Society**

The Beginnings of Civilization

A. As You Read

Directions: As you read Section 3, fill in the table below with information about developments in early human society.

Steps in the Rise of Civilizations

Development	How It Changed Human Society
Farming and Raising Animals	1.
Growth of Population	2.
Rise of Cities	3.
Trade	4.
Social Classes	5.

B. Reviewing Key Terms

Directions: On a separate sheet of paper, write the definitions for the following key terms.

6. irrigation

7. surplus

8. artisan

9. civilization

10. social class

GUIDED READING AND REVIEW

Land Between Two Rivers

A. As You Read

Directions: As you read Section 1, fill in the table below with details about Mesopotamia and the civilizations that developed there.

Facts About Mesopotamia

Location	1.
Important Geographic Features	2.
Ways of Life	3.
Religion	4.

B. Reviewing Key Terms

Directions: Complete each sentence by writing the correct term in the blank provided.

5. In ancient Sumer, if a person wanted a letter written or a list of trade items drawn up, he or she would hire a professional writer called a __________________ .

6. The belief in many gods is called __________________ .

7. Stories about gods are also known as __________________ .

8. In ancient Mesopotamia, each __________________ acted as a state with its own ruler.

CHAPTER 2
The Fertile Crescent

Babylonia and Assyria

A. As You Read

Directions: As you read Section 2, fill in the table below with details about the rise of Babylonia and Assyria.

Rise of Empires in the Fertile Crescent

1750 B.C.	600s B.C.	612 B.C.	539 B.C.
1.	2.	3.	4.

B. Reviewing Key Terms

Directions: In the blanks provided, write the definitions for the following key terms.

5. empire

____

____

6. caravan

____

____

7. bazaar

____

____

GUIDED READING AND REVIEW

The Legacy of Mesopotamia

CHAPTER 2
The Fertile Crescent

A. As You Read

Directions: As you read Section 3, fill in the table below with information about Mesopotamian civilization. Under each main idea, write two supporting statements.

Main Idea A
The rules set down by Hammurabi were an important step in the development of civilization in Mesopotamia.

1. ____

____

2. ____

____

Main Idea B
Writing was one of the major breakthroughs for the civilizations of Mesopotamia.

3. ____

____

4. ____

____

____

B. Reviewing Key Terms

Directions: Complete each sentence by writing the correct term in the blank provided.

5. An organized list of laws is also called a __________________ .

6. Writing in Mesopotamia combined symbols to make groups of wedges and lines known

as __________________

CHAPTER 2
The Fertile Crescent

Mediterranean Civilizations

A. As You Read

Directions: As you read Section 4, fill in the table below with information about the Phoenicians and Israelites.

Civilizations of the Phoenicians and Israelites

	Phoenicia	Israel
Location	1.	2.
Main City or Cities	3.	4.
Ways of Life	5.	6.
Main Achievements	7.	8.

B. Key Terms

Directions: Complete each sentence by writing the correct term in the blank provided.

9. A set of symbols that represent the sounds of a language is called a(n)

_____________________ .

10. The Assyrians _____________________ the Israelites by sending them into distant parts of their empire.

11. A time when there is so little food that many people starve is known as

a(n)_____________________ .

12. Belief in one God is called _____________________ .

GUIDED READING AND REVIEW

Judaism

A. As You Read

Directions: As you read Section 5, complete the statements below.

1. The early Israelites recorded events and laws in a text that is called __________________ .

2. Most ancient peoples thought that their gods were connected with certain places or people. However, the Israelites believed that God was __________________ .

3. The laws that Israelites believe God gave them through Moses are called the __________________ .

4. Early in Israelite history, a judge named __________________ won honor and respect.

5. Unlike many ancient peoples, the early Israelites thought of their rulers as human instead of as __________________ .

6. The Romans drove the Israelites out of their homeland in the year __________________ .

7. Judaism had an important influence on these two later religions: __________________ and __________________ .

B. Reviewing Key Terms

Directions: In the blanks provided, write the definitions for the following key terms.

8. covenant

____

____

9. prophet

____

____

10. diaspora

____

____

The Geography of the Nile

A. As You Read

Directions: As you read Section 1, complete the statements below.

1. An early description of the Nile was written by the Greek historian _______________ .

2. The direction that the Nile River flows is _______________ to the Mediterranean Sea from its sources in Africa.

3. The Blue Nile and White Nile meet at the city of _______________ , in the present-day country of Sudan.

4. The marshy region of the Nile near the Mediterranean Sea is known as

   _______________ Egypt.

5. The ancient Egyptians called their land _______________ , "the black land," because of the dark soil left by the Nile's floods.

6. Deserts to the east and west protected the Egyptians from _______________ by foreign enemies.

7. Communities appeared in the Nile delta of Lower Egypt by around _______________ .

B. Reviewing Key Terms

Directions: Complete each sentence by writing the correct term in the blank provided.

8. Water from the Nile River deposited rich, fertile soil called _______________ when the river overflowed its banks.

9. In the Nubian section of the Nile, the river contains many rock-filled rapids, or

   _______________ .

10. The _______________ of the Nile, a triangle-shaped area of very rich farmland, is located in Lower Egypt.

Egypt's Powerful Kings and Queens

A. As You Read

Directions: As you read Section 2, fill in the table below with information about Egypt's ancient rulers. Under each main idea, write two supporting details.

Main Idea A
The rulers of the Old Kingdom paved the way for Egypt's long history as one of the most stable societies in the ancient world.

1. ____

2. ____

Main Idea B
The able rulers of the New Kingdom built an empire.

3. ____

4. ____

B. Reviewing Key Terms

Directions: Complete each sentence by writing the correct term in the blank provided.

5. The ancient Egyptians' name for their king was _________________ .

6. During its long history, ancient Egypt was governed by 31 different ruling families called _________________ .

7. Someone who rules for a child until the child is old enough to rule is called a _________________ .

Egyptian Religion

A. As You Read

Directions: As you read Section 3, fill in the table below with information about ancient Egyptian religion.

Religious Beliefs of the Ancient Egyptians

Egyptian God	Description
Amon-Re	1.
Osiris	2.
Isis	3.

Directions: Use the information in Section 3 to describe how to build a pyramid in four or five steps. If you need more space, write the steps on the back of this page or on another sheet of paper.

4. ____

____

____

____

B. Reviewing Key Terms

Directions: On a separate sheet of paper, write the definitions for the following key terms.

5. afterlife   7. pyramid

6. mummy

The Culture of the Ancient Egyptians

A. As You Read

Directions: As you read Section 4, fill in the pyramid below with information about Egyptian social classes. On each level of the pyramid, write the name and a brief description of the appropriate class.

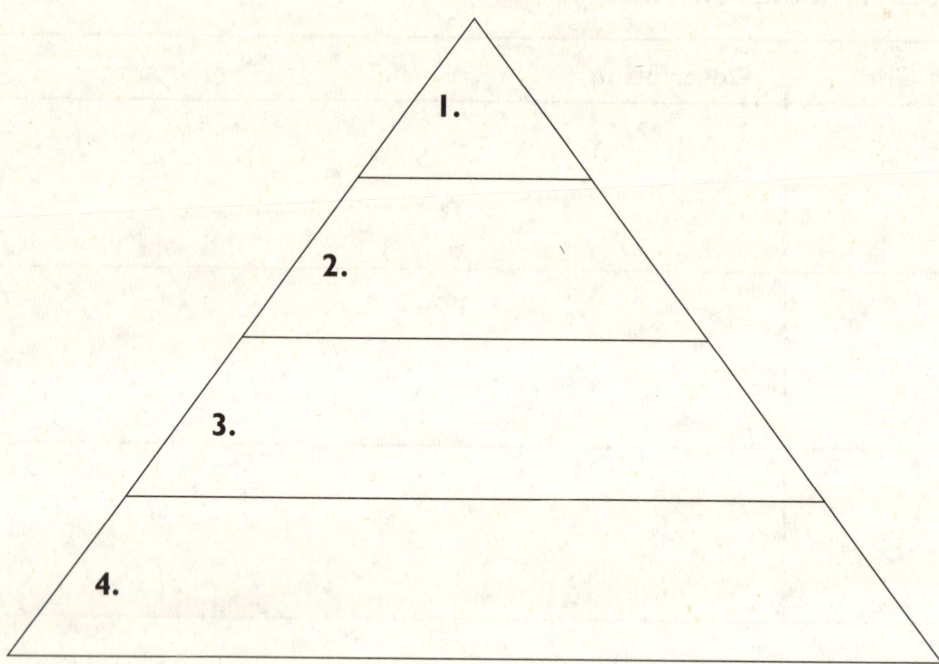

B. Reviewing Key Terms

Directions: In the blanks provided, write the definitions for the following key terms.

5. hieroglyph

____

____

6. papyrus

____

____

7. astronomer

____

____

CHAPTER 3
Ancient Egypt and Nubia

The Resource-Rich Cultures of Nubia

A. As You Read

Directions: As you read Section 5, fill in the table below with information about the three ancient Nubian kingdoms.

Three Nubian Kingdoms

Nubian Kingdom	Location	Achievements
1.	2.	3.
4.	5.	6.
7.	8.	9.

B. Reviewing Key Terms

Directions: In the blank provided, write the definition for the following key term.

10. artisan

____

____

GUIDED READING AND REVIEW

The Indus and Ganges River Valleys

CHAPTER 4
Ancient India

A. As You Read

Directions: As you read Section 1, complete the statements below.

1. The natural barrier that separates India from the rest of Asia is the _______________________ .

2. The earliest people of northern India probably entered the Indus Valley from passes in the _______________________ mountain range.

3. One of India's earliest cities, located along the banks of the Indus River, was

_______________________ .

4. The earliest known religious books of Aryan society are the _______________________ .

5. The four social classes that emerged in early Aryan society were the

____

____ .

B. Reviewing Key Terms

Directions: Complete each sentence by writing the correct term in the blank provided.

6. In the center of Mohenjo-Daro, there was a fortress consisting of a group of public

buildings. Another name for this fortress is a _______________________ .

7. During the summer, seasonal winds called _______________________ blow moist air across India from the Indian Ocean.

8. The strict division of classes that began in India around 500 B.C. is known as the

_______________________ system.

9. A large landmass that juts out from a continent is called a _______________________ .

10. The Aryans moved, or _______________________ , into the Indus Valley around 1500 B.C.

<table>
<tr><td>**CHAPTER 4**
Ancient India</td><td># The Beginnings of Hinduism</td><td></td></tr>
</table>

A. As You Read

Directions: As you read Section 2, complete the statements below.

1. As Hinduism developed over the years, it absorbed many beliefs from other

____________________ .

2. Over the years, there have been many Hindu religious thinkers, but Hinduism has no

single ____________________ .

3. The gods and goddesses of Hinduism stand for different parts of a single

____________________ .

4. The three most important Hindu gods are ____________________ , ____________________ ,

and ____________________ .

5. One of the important texts of Hinduism is the ____________________ , which is mostly in
the form of questions and answers between pupils and teachers.

Directions: Answer the following questions in the space provided.

6. According to Hinduism, what happens to people who have been bad during their life after
they die?

____

____

7. According to Hinduism, how can a person be freed from the cycle of death and rebirth?

____

B. Reviewing Key Terms

Directions: Complete each sentence by writing the correct term in the blank provided.

8. The Hindu belief that souls are reborn in the body of another living thing is known as

____________________ .

9. Many Hindus believe in the idea of ____________________ , or nonviolence.

10. In Hinduism, the religious and moral duties of each person are called ____________________ .

11. Hindus worship many gods and goddesses called ____________________ .

GUIDED READING AND REVIEW

The Beginnings of Buddhism

A. As You Read

Directions: As you read Section 3, complete the statements below.

1. Gautama's dissatisfaction with the teachings of __________________ led him to a set of new beliefs.

2. The followers of Gautama called him "The Enlightened One," or __________________ .

3. Gautama taught that suffering is caused by ____

____ .

4. According to Gautama, the way to become free from suffering is to follow the

__________________ .

5. Gautama taught that all people are __________________ , regardless of their social class.

6. The Golden Age of Buddhism came during the reign of __________________ , one of India's greatest rulers.

7. Many Hindus came to honor Gautama as a reincarnation of the god __________________ .

B. Reviewing Key Terms

Directions: In the blanks provided, write the definitions for the following key terms.

8. meditate

____

____

9. nirvana

____

____

10. missionary

____

____

CHAPTER 4
Ancient India

The Golden Age of Maurya India

A. As You Read

Directions: As you read Section 4, fill in the table below with events that took place during the Maurya rule of India.

The Maurya Empire

330 B.C.	261 B.C.	232 B.C.
1.	2.	3.

B. Reviewing Key Terms

Directions: Complete each sentence by writing the correct term in the blank provided.

4. Chandragupta believed that a ruler must have complete control, or _________________, over the people.

5. After the great slaughter at Kalinga, Asoka changed his beliefs, or _________________, to Buddhism.

GUIDED READING AND REVIEW

The Geography of China's River Valleys

A. As You Read

Directions: As you read Section 1, complete the statements below.

1. To survive in the dry land in northern China called the _______________ , people have always depended on rivers.

2. The Huang He, or _______________ , begins in the highlands of Tibet.

3. Early Chinese civilization started around 5000 B.C., when the people gave up their wandering way of life and began _______________ .

4. In ancient China, the most important part of society was not the state but the

   _______________ .

5. A household in ancient China might contain as many as _______________ generations living together.

6. According to tradition in ancient China, men had a higher status than

   _______________ .

7. When a father died, all his lands were divided among his _______________ .

B. Reviewing Key Terms

Directions: In the blanks provided, write the definitions for the following key terms.

8. loess

   ____

9. dike

   ____

10. extended family

    ____

    ____

Confucius and His Teachings

A. As You Read

Directions: As you read Section 2, fill in the table below with information about Confucianism.

The Teachings of Confucius

A Person's Place in the Family and Society	**1.**
The Golden Rule	**2.**

Directions: As you read Section 2, explain how the teachings of Confucius helped shape Chinese government. Use the spaces provided below.

3. ____

____

____

____

____

____

____

B. Reviewing Key Terms

Directions: Complete each sentence by writing the correct term in the blank provided.

4. A group of people who carry out the day-to-day work of the government is the

______________________ .

5. A system of beliefs and values is also known as a ______________________ .

GUIDED READING AND REVIEW

Strong Rulers Unite Warring Kingdoms

A. As You Read

Directions: As you read Section 3, fill in the table below with facts about China's dynasties.

Some Facts About China's Dynasties

Ruler	Dynasty Name	Main Accomplishments
Shi Huangdi	1.	2.
Liu Bang	3.	4.
Wudi	5.	6.

B. Reviewing Key Terms

Directions: In the blanks provided, write the definitions for the following key terms.

7. currency

____

____

8. warlord

____

____

CHAPTER 5
Ancient China

Achievements of Ancient China

A. As You Read

Directions: As you read Section 4, fill in the table below with information about the legacy of ancient China. Under each main idea, write two supporting statements.

Main Idea A
China became known to the West as a result of the Silk Road.

1. ____

____

2. ____

____

Main Idea B
The Chinese inventions of the Han dynasty are still with us today.

3. ____

____

4. ____

____

B. Reviewing Key Terms

Directions: Complete the sentence by writing the correct term in the blank provided.

5. A valuable cloth made only in China in ancient times was _______________ .

The Rise of Greek Civilization

A. As You Read

Directions: As you read Section 1, answer the following questions in the space provided.

1. How would you describe the islands of Greece?

____

2. How did Greece's landforms influence the way of life of the people living there?

____

3. According to Greek legend, what event started the Trojan War?

____

4. What period of time has been called Greece's Dark Ages?

____

5. Which Greek city became the center for a new system of government in which citizens governed themselves?

____

B. Reviewing Key Terms

Directions: Complete each sentence by writing the correct term in the blank provided.

6. Members of rich and powerful families who rule communities are known as

_____________________ .

7. The *Iliad* and the *Odyssey,* long poems about the Trojan War and its aftermath, are

examples of _____________________ .

8. A piece of land surrounded by water on three sides is known as a(n)

_____________________ .

9. In ancient Greece, independent communities that followed their own traditions, government,

and laws came to be known as _____________________ .

10. An early Greek settlement on a high, rocky hill is called a(n) _____________________ .

11. A form of government in which citizens govern themselves is known as a(n)

_____________________ .

12. In ancient Greece, rulers who were supported by the middle and working classes were

called _____________________ .

Greek Religion, Philosophy, and Literature

A. As You Read

Directions: As you read Section 2, fill in the table below with information about the Golden Age of Athens.

Athens During Its Golden Age

Years of the Golden Age	**1.**
Main Political Leader	**2.**
Artistic Accomplishments of Athens	**3.**

Directions: In the space provided, write one statement about each Greek thinker.

4. Thales

____

5. Democritus

____

6. Socrates

____

B. Reviewing Key Terms

Directions: Complete each sentence by writing the correct term in the blank provided.

7. A serious play that often ends in disaster for the main character is called a

_______________________ .

8. A person who uses the power of his or her mind and reason to understand natural events

is called a _________________________ .

9. The ancient Greeks believed that their gods were _________________________ , which means they lived forever.

10. Cities in the Athenian empire paid _________________________ to Athens, adding to its wealth.

Daily Life of the Ancient Greeks

A. As You Read

Directions: As you read Section 3, fill in the table below with information about the daily lives of the ancient Greeks. Under each main idea, write two supporting statements.

Main Idea A
The marketplace of Athens was the liveliest place in the city-state.

1. ____

2. ____

Main Idea B
Slavery was a fact of life in ancient Greece.

3. ____

4. ____

B. Reviewing Key Terms

Directions: Complete the sentence below by writing the correct term in the blank.

5. The public market and meeting place in an ancient Greek city was called the

_______________________ .

GUIDED READING AND REVIEW

CHAPTER 6
Ancient Greece

Athens and Sparta:
Two Cities in Conflict

A. As You Read

Directions: As you read Section 4, fill in the table with information about Sparta and Athens. Look back at Sections 1–3 to find additional information about Athens.

Two Different City-States

	Sparta	Athens
Main Way of Life	1.	2.
Role of Citizens	3.	4.
Role of Women	5.	6.
Attitude Toward Art and Learning	7.	8.

B. Reviewing Key Terms

In the blanks provided below, write the definitions for the following key terms.

9. plague

____

____

10. blockade

____

____

The Spread of Greek Culture

A. As You Read

Directions: As you read Section 5, fill in the table below with information about King Philip and Alexander the Great.

338 B.C.	332 B.C.	323 B.C.
1.	2.	3.

Directions: Briefly describe the accomplishments of the following people.

4. Euclid

____

5. Eratosthenes

____

6. Archimedes

____

B. Reviewing Key Terms

Directions: Complete each sentence by writing the correct term in the blank provided.

7. Athenians thought of Macedonians as _______________ , or uncivilized people.

8. Alexander came to the throne of Macedonia after his father was _______________ .

9. When Alexander took control of lands, he made them _______________ by blending local cultures with Greek ways.

CHAPTER 7
Ancient Rome

The Roman Republic

A. As You Read

Directions: As you read Section 1, answer the following questions in the space provided.

1. On which peninsula is Rome located?

____

2. When did people first settle in Rome?

____

3. Which mysterious people conquered the Romans around 600 B.C.?

____

4. What was the form of government established by the Romans after they drove out the last Etruscan king?

____

5. Which empire was destroyed as a result of Rome's invasion of North Africa?

____

6. Who became dictator of the Roman world in 44 B.C.?

____

B. Reviewing Key Terms

Directions: Complete each sentence by writing the correct term in the blank provided.

7. In Rome, ordinary citizens were called _______________________ .

8. In the senate, the power was held by men from the wealthy classes, called

_______________________ .

9. In times of emergency, Romans could appoint a _______________________ , who was given the powers of a king but could rule for only six months.

10. The word _______________________ comes from the Latin term meaning "I forbid it."

11. In Rome, two men called _______________________ ruled the government and had the power to veto each other's actions.

12. A form of government in which citizens elect leaders to rule in the name of the people

is a _______________________ .

The Roman Empire

A. As You Read

Directions: As you read Section 2, fill in the table below with information about imperial Rome. Under each main idea, write two supporting statements.

Main Idea A
The first Roman emperor, Augustus, set an example for skillful rule that allowed the empire to flourish.

1. ____

____

2. ____

____

Main Idea B
Two of Rome's greatest achievements were in the areas of architecture and law.

3. ____

____

4. ____

____

B. Reviewing Key Terms

Directions: In the blanks provided, write the definitions for the following key terms.

5. province

____

____

6. aqueduct

____

____

Daily Life Among the Romans

A. As You Read

Directions: As you read Section 3, fill in the table below with facts about life in Rome.

How the Ancient Romans Lived

Ancient Romans	How They Lived
The Wealthy	1.
The Poor	2.
Slaves	3.
Women	4.

B. Reviewing Key Terms

Directions: Complete the sentence below by writing the correct term in the blank provided.

5. Along with free grain, the emperors also provided poor Romans with huge entertainment

events called __________________ .

A New Religion: Christianity

A. As You Read

Directions: As you read Section 4, fill in the table below.

Facts About Christianity

Where It Started	**1.**
When It Started	**2.**
How the Religion Spread	**3.**
Persecution of Followers	**4.**

B. Reviewing Key Terms

Directions: In the blanks provided, write the definitions for the following key terms.

5. martyr

____

6. disciple

____

7. epistle

____

8. Gospel

____

9. messiah

____

CHAPTER 7
Ancient Rome

The Fall of Rome

A. As You Read

Directions: As you read Section 5, complete the table below with information about the fall of Rome.

A.D. 180   A.D. 330   A.D. 410

1.	2.	3.

Directions: In the space provided, describe how each concept contributed to the decline of Rome's power.

4. Weak, Corrupt Rulers

____

____

5. Use of Foreign Soldiers

____

____

B. Reviewing Key Terms

Directions: Complete each sentence by writing the correct term in the blank provided.

6. Soldiers who fight for a country in return for pay are called _______________ .

7. An economic situation known as _______________ occurs when the value of a country's money decreases.

GUIDED READING AND REVIEW

Byzantium
Rome's Eastern Empire

A. As You Read

Directions: As you read Section 1, answer the following questions on a separate sheet of paper.

1. What did the Byzantines use to defend their capital against attacks? What did it contain?

2. Why was Constantinople an important city?

3. What person was Constantinople named after? Why was he important?

4. Why did the Byzantine empire last longer than the western Roman Empire?

5. Why was Justinian not a typical emperor?

6. What argument sparked the fall of the Byzantine empire?

7. Who took over Constantinople in 1453?

8. What are two achievements of the Byzantines?

B. Reviewing Key Terms

Directions: Complete each sentence by writing the correct term in the blank provided.

9. Constantinople lay on the _____________________ called the Bosporus.

10. Early medieval Christians disagreed about the worship of _____________________ .

11. The leader of the Byzantine Church was called the _____________________ .

12. The _____________________ between Rome and Constantinople eventually led to the fall of the Byzantine empire.

The Rise and Spread of Islam

A. As You Read

Directions: As you read Section 2, fill in the table below with details about the rise and spread of Islam.

The Rise and Spread of Islam

Geography of the Arabian Peninsula	1.
Bedouins and Merchants	2. 3.
Muhammad	4. 5.
Hijra	6. 7.
Spread of Islam	8. 9.

B. Reviewing Key Terms

Directions: For each definition below, write the key term on a separate sheet of paper.

10. a person who moves from place to place and has no permanent home

11. someone who claims to carry the word of God

12. the move by Muhammad and his followers from Mecca to Yathrib in 622

GUIDED READING AND REVIEW

The Religion of Islam

CHAPTER I
The Byzantine and Muslim Empires

A. As You Read

Directions: As you read Section 3, fill in the chart below with information about the religion of Islam.

Muslim Beliefs	**1.** **2.**
Islam and Other Religions	**3.** **4.**
Men's and Women's Roles	**5.**
Sunni and Shiite Schism	**6.** **7.**

B. Reviewing Key Terms

Directions: Complete the sentences below by writing the key term in the blank provided.

8. Five times each day, _____________________ throughout the Islamic world call Muslims to prayer.

9. The Muslim house of worship is called a _____________________ .

10. During _____________________ , Muslims must fast during daylight hours.

11. Muslims from all over the world come to Mecca each year for the _____________________ .

12. Muslims can find stories, promises, warnings, and rules for daily life in the

_____________________ .

Islam's Golden Age

A. As You Read

Directions: As you read Section 4, complete the statements below.

1. The period between 800 and 1100 is known as Islam's ____________________ .

2. One of the reasons that artists and scientists had time to work was that the Muslim empire had plenty of ____________________ .

3. The capital of the Muslim empire during Islam's golden age was ____________________ .

4. For 23 years, Harun ar-Rashid, caliph of Baghdad, ruled the world's ____________________ .

5. The Muslim empire benefited from its policy of ____________________ toward people of all religions.

6. Maimonides tried to explain how people could believe in ____________________ and ____________________ at the same time.

7. Muslim scholars made lasting contributions to ____________________ , ____________________ , and ____________________ .

8. Sufis were Muslims who used poetry to teach ideas and ____________________ .

9. Jalal ad-Din ar-Rumi founded a group known in the West as the ____________________ .

B. Reviewing Key Terms

Directions: For each key term below, write the definition in the blank provided.

10. caliph

____

11. patron

____

12. tolerance

____

GUIDED READING AND REVIEW

The Bantu Migrations

A. As You Read

Directions: As you read Section 1, fill in the tables below with information about the physical features of Africa and the Bantu migrations.

Physical Features of Africa

Vegetation	1.
	2.
Landforms	3.
	4.

Bantu Migrations

Who, When, Where	5.
	6.
Impact on Africa	7.
	8.

B. Reviewing Key Terms

Directions: For each definition below, write the key term in the blank provided.

9. rolling grassland in Africa _____________________

10. a place in a desert that has water and vegetation _____________________

11. movement of people from place to place _____________________

12. a group of families who have the same ancestor _____________________

CHAPTER 2
Civilizations of Africa

Kingdoms of West Africa

A. As You Read

Directions: As you read Section 2, answer the following questions in the space provided.

1. How did African kingdoms like Mali become rich?

____

____

2. What items were the heart of trade in West Africa?

____

3. What was the first West African trade empire? About when did it begin to control trade routes?

____

4. What were some of the products traded in Ghana?

____

5. When was Mali founded? What thing other than trade helped to make Mali rich?

____

6. Who was Mansa Musa? What are two ways in which he changed the empire of Mali?

____

____

7. For what was Tombouctou best known?

____

8. What happened to Mali after the death of Mansa Musa?

____

9. What was the leading state in West Africa by the end of the 1400s?

____

B. Reviewing Key Terms

Directions: Complete each sentence by writing the correct term in the blank provided.

10. When gold and salt traders met, they used _________________ to conduct their business.

11. Many _________________ in Mali became independent when the empire weakened.

GUIDED READING AND REVIEW

Trading States of East Africa

A. As You Read

Directions: As you read Section 3, complete the statements below.

1. Some historians believe that the kingdom of Sheba is actually the land called

   ___________________ .

2. Two groups who settled along the coast of northeastern Africa were the

   ___________________ and the ___________________ .

3. Aksum was on the trade route between ___________________ and the

   ___________________ .

4. During the A.D. 300s, Aksum's king became a ___________________ .

5. When Christians from Aksum were forced to move by Muslims, they settled in

   ___________________ .

6. By 1200, there were about ___________________ city-states along the eastern coast of Africa.

7. Kilwa was a ___________________ city on an island off the East African coast.

8. Swahili is a ___________________ language with borrowed ___________________ words.

9. Beginning in the 1500s, armies from ___________________ captured Kilwa and other Swahili cities, but Swahili culture remains to this day.

10. Great Zimbabwe was an interior kingdom founded by a group of Bantu-speaking people called the ___________________ .

B. Reviewing Key Terms

Directions: For each definition below, write the key term in the blank provided.

11. a city that has its own government and controls the lands around it ___________________

12. the language and culture of many of the people of East Africa ___________________

CHAPTER 3
The Ancient Americas

Cultures of Middle America

A. As You Read

Directions: As you read Section 1, fill in the table below with details about the cultures of the Mayan and the Aztec people. Write one or two items for each number.

The Mayas	
Farming	**1.**
Religion	**2.**
Achievements	**3.**
The Aztecs	
Tenochtitlán	**4.**
Way of Life	**5.**
Society and Religion	**6.**

B. Reviewing Key Terms

Directions: In the blanks provided, write the definitions for the following key terms.

7. maize ____

8. slash-and-burn agriculture _______________________________

9. hieroglyphs ____

10. causeway ____

11. aqueduct ____

12. artisan ____

CHAPTER 3
The Ancient
Americas

The Incas

A. As You Read

Directions: As you read Section 2, complete the statements below.

1. The Incas depended on _____________________ to carry messages to and from the capital at Cuzco.

2. In the Incan system of government, the emperor was the only person who owned the

   _____________________ .

3. All people in the Incan empire were expected to pay _____________________ .

4. The Incan government took care of the _____________________ , the

   _____________________ , and the _____________________ .

5. In order for messengers to travel, the Incas built a vast system of _____________________

   and _____________________ .

6. Incan roads allowed the _____________________ to travel quickly in times of trouble.

7. Without any modern power tools, the Incas built huge _____________________ .

8. When the Incas built a _____________________ , the fit of the stones was so tight that not even a very thin knife blade could be slipped between them.

9. The ancient stone buildings of Cuzco have withstood major storms and earthquakes for

   _____________________ .

10. The Incas increased their farmland by building a system of _____________________ and

    _____________________ and by cutting _____________________ into mountainsides.

B. Reviewing Key Terms

Directions: In the blanks provided, write the key terms for the following definitions.

11. knotted strings used by the Incas to record information about taxes, births, deaths, and

    harvests _____________________

12. a ledge cut into a mountainside and used for growing crops _____________________

© Pearson Education, Inc.

CHAPTER 3
The Ancient Americas

Cultures of North America

A. As You Read

Directions: As you read Section 3, answer the questions below in the space provided.

1. When did the Native Americans called the Mound Builders live?

____

2. What was Cahokia? Where was it located?

____

3. How were most of the mounds in Cahokia shaped? How were they built?

____

4. What was the purpose of the great serpent mound in Ohio?

____

5. What items have researchers found in serpent mounds?

____

6. What did researchers notice about some of the items that they found in serpent mounds?

____

7. What does the word Anasazi mean?

____

8. In what region did the Anasazi people settle?

____

9. What crops did the Anasazi grow? How did they bring water to dry farmlands?

____

10. Why did the Anasazi build their villages into steep cliffs or on top of mesas?

____

11. When the Pueblo people wanted to please rain spirits, what did they do?

____

B. Reviewing Key Terms

Directions: Complete the sentence by writing the correct term in the blank provided.

12. The Anasazi people of the Southwest built villages called __________________ into the side of steep cliffs.

GUIDED READING AND REVIEW

Golden Ages in China

A. As You Read

Directions: As you read Section 1, fill in the table below with information about ancient China. Under each main idea, write several supporting details.

Main Idea A
The ideas of Confucius influenced Chinese government during the Tang and Song dynasties.

1. ____

____

2. ____

____

Main Idea B
The Tang and Song dynasties are called the golden ages for culture and trade in China.

3. ____

____

4. ____

____

5. ____

____

6. ____

____

B. Reviewing Key Terms

Directions: In the blanks provided, write the definitions for the following key terms.

7. dynasty ____

8. merit system ____

9. porcelain ____

10. movable type ____

CHAPTER 4
Civilizations of Asia

Feudalism in Japan

A. As You Read

Directions: As you read Section 2, answer the following questions on a separate sheet of paper.

1. What does the word *samurai* mean?

2. What happened in Japan as the daimyo gained power?

3. What took place during the rule of weak shoguns?

4. How did the landing of Portuguese sailors in 1543 affect life in Japan?

5. Why did Tokugawa Ieyasu isolate Japan from Westerners?

6. How did the shoguns keep Japan isolated?

7. For how long did Japan's isolation last?

B. Reviewing Key Terms

Directions: Complete the sentences below by writing the correct terms in the blanks provided.

8. Japanese warriors who worked for and were very loyal to estate owners were called

   _______________________ .

9. In Japan, the _______________________ , or estate owners, became very powerful and independent.

10. The Japanese code of rules that stresses honor, discipline, bravery, and simple living

    is called _______________________ .

11. The most powerful group of people in the Japanese _______________________ was the daimyo.

12. The person who controlled Japan in the emperor's name was called the

    _______________________ .

GUIDED READING AND REVIEW

The Great Mughal Empire in India

A. As You Read

Directions: As you read Section 3, complete the statements below.

1. India had always been called a land of ___________________ .

2. Hindus accepted many gods, who they believed were aspects of one

   ___________________ .

3. India's golden age under the Gupta dynasty ended when different groups

   ___________________ the empire.

4. The Turkish prince Babur founded the ___________________ empire, which lasted into the 1700s.

5. Akbar realized that the best way to make the empire peaceful was to be fair to people

   of different ___________________ .

6. Akbar regularly brought together ___________________ of different religions for discussion.

7. Even though Akbar himself had never learned to read or write, he supported

   ___________________ .

8. More than 100 years after Akbar's death, the Mughal empire began to fall apart because

   rulers began to spend too much money on ___________________ and

   ___________________ .

9. Shah Jahan is best known for constructing the ___________________ as a tomb for his dead wife.

B. Reviewing Key Terms

Directions: In the blank provided, write the key term for each definition.

10. a religion and a way of life that developed in India over a long period of time

    ____

11. a Hindu system under which people are divided into strict social classes

    ____

12. the Muslim king of the empire that included what is today India, Bangladesh, and

    Pakistan ___________________

Feudalism: A System for Living

A. As You Read

Directions: As you read Section 1, fill in the chart with information about the beginnings of feudalism. Write several facts for each item listed.

Collapse of the Roman Empire	**1.**
Charlemagne	**2.**
Need for Feudalism	**3.**
Feudal System	**4.**

B. Reviewing Key Terms

Directions: Complete these sentences by writing the correct terms in the blanks provided.

5. The period in Europe between A.D. 500 and 1500 is known as the ___________________ .

6. One of the great kings during ___________________ times in Europe was Charlemagne.

7. Under the system of ___________________ , kings and queens had the most power, lords were next, then came vassals, and finally serfs.

8. The men who swore loyalty to a lord and were given land in return were called

___________________ .

9. A lord's ___________________ was a large estate that often included the surrounding farmland and a village.

10. The people of a medieval manor had to be ___________________ because they usually lived far from other towns and villages.

11. When a lord was given a manor, the ___________________ who lived there became his as well.

The Rise of Cities

A. As You Read

Directions: As you read Section 2, fill in the table below with information about elements of life in medieval Europe.

Life in Europe During the Middle Ages

Power of the Church	**1.**
Merchant Class	**2.**
Growth of Towns	**3.**
Guilds	**4.**
Disease	**5.**
Culture and Learning	**6.**

B. Reviewing Key Terms

Directions: In the blank provided, write the correct key term for each definition below.

   7. persons ordained to perform certain religious duties ______________________

   8. to prevent someone from taking part in Church life ______________________

   9. an association of all the people in a town who practice a certain trade ______________________

 10. an unpaid worker who is being trained in a craft ______________________

 11. the noble qualities that knights were supposed to have ______________________

 12. a traveling performer who sang about the deeds of knights ______________________

CHAPTER 5
Europe in the Middle Ages

The Crusades

A. As You Read

Directions: As you read Section 3, answer the following questions on a separate sheet of paper.

1. What reasons did Pope Urban II give for attacking the Seljuk Turks in the Holy Land?

2. For how long did the Crusades last?

3. What is the Holy Land? Why is it an important area?

4. For what reasons did Christian pilgrims travel to the Holy Land?

5. What was a nonreligious reason for the Crusades?

6. What did Peter the Hermit do before the First Crusade? What happened to the people who followed him?

7. Why did the Byzantines regret asking for help from the Europeans?

8. What happened when the crusaders of the First Crusade captured Jerusalem in 1099?

9. What happened after the First Crusade?

10. How did the Muslims react to the Christian kingdoms in the Holy Land?

11. What was an important way in which the Crusades changed Europe?

B. Reviewing Key Terms

Directions: Complete the sentence below by writing the correct term in the blank provided.

12. During the _____________________ , the Catholic Church sent armies to the Holy Land to fight the Seljuk Turks.

Kings and Popes

A. As You Read

Directions: As you read Section 4, complete the statements below.

1. In the Middle Ages, kings and popes often quarreled over who should pick Church officials called _______________ .

2. As European kings gained power, they dared to put their own wishes before those of the _______________ .

3. One of the ways in which kings became more powerful was that they hired _______________ with money paid by townspeople for protection.

4. King John of England was unpopular because he _______________ people heavily and jailed his enemies whenever he wished.

5. The Hundred Years' War was fought between England and _______________ .

6. Edward III of England thought that he should be the _______________ of France.

7. Joan of Arc defeated the English at _______________ and four other locations.

8. When the English captured Joan of Arc, they tried her as a _______________ and burned her at the stake.

B. Reviewing Key Terms

Directions: In the blank provided, write the definition for each key term below.

9. nation

____

10. Magna Carta

____

11. Parliament

____

CHAPTER 6
A New Age in Europe

The Renaissance and Reformation

A. As You Read

Directions: As you read Section 1, fill in the table below with information about the Renaissance and the Reformation. Write three details that support each main idea.

Main Idea A
The Renaissance was a rebirth of learning and the arts that began in northern Italy.
I. ____
2. ____
3. ____
Main Idea B
The Reformation was begun by Martin Luther and led to the formation of the Protestant Church.
4. ____
5. ____
6. ____

B. Reviewing Key Terms

Directions: Write the correct key term for each definition below.

7. a 300-year period when Europe experienced a rebirth in learning and culture

____

8. a painting technique in which an artist shows objects as they appear to the eye, for example, by making distant objects smaller in relation to closer objects _______________________

9. the change or reform of the Catholic Church begun by Martin Luther in Germany

____

10. an official pardon for sins given by the pope in return for money _______________________

11. a person who held similar views to Martin Luther, whose religion grew out of protest against Roman Catholicism _______________________

The Age of Exploration

A. As You Read

Directions: As you read Section 2, answer the following questions on a separate sheet of paper.

1. Why did European countries search for new trade routes to Asia?

2. What were some of the advances that the Portuguese made in sailing under Prince Henry's leadership?

3. What accomplishment did Vasco da Gama achieve?

4. How did the Spanish contribute to ocean exploration?

5. What plan did Ferdinand Magellan have when he set sail?

6. Where is the Strait of Magellan? How long did it take Magellan to sail through the strait?

7. What happened to Magellan in the Philippines?

8. How many of Magellan's original five ships returned to Spain? How many sailors? What had they accomplished?

B. Reviewing Key Terms

Directions: In the blanks provided, write the definitions for the following key terms.

9. navigator

____

10. caravel

____

11. astrolabe

____

12. circumnavigate

____

CHAPTER 6
**A New Age
in Europe**

The Age of Powerful Kings

A. As You Read

Directions: As you read Section 3, fill in the table below with information about the age of powerful kings in Europe. Write two ideas for each category below.

Kings in Europe

Divine Right of Kings	**I.** **2.**
Absolute Monarchy	**3.** **4.**
The Court of the Sun King	**5.** **6.**
Other European Monarchs	**7.** **8.**

B. Reviewing Key Terms

Directions: Complete each sentence by writing the correct term in the blank provided.

9. The idea of a government being run by the people, or a _____________________ , was unheard of in the time of Louis XIV.

10. Louis XIV believed that he ruled through _____________________ , or by the choice of God.

11. An _____________________ controls every aspect of life in his or her kingdom.

4

Conquests in the Americas and Africa

A. As You Read

Directions: As you read Section 4, complete the statements below.

1. When the Spanish conquistadors landed, the Aztecs wondered whether one of them, Cortés, could be the god _______________ .

2. After Cortés arrived in Mexico, a Native American woman named Malinche told him about the _______________ of the Aztecs.

3. When Cortés first arrived in Tenochtitlán, Moctezuma _______________ him.

4. After the final battle of Tenochtitlán, the Aztec empire lay in _______________ .

5. Under the encomienda system, landlords were supposed to _______________ Native Americans, but they did not.

6. Francisco Pizarro was able to conquer the Incas with a few soldiers because a _______________ was raging in the Incan empire.

7. Europeans traded in Africa for _______________ , _______________ , and _______________ .

8. Though there was no market for _______________ in Europe, there was a market in the Americas.

9. Some historians think that about _______________ enslaved Africans were brought to the Americas and that an equal number may have died on the journey.

10. While some Africans grew wealthy from the slave trade, overall it was a _______________ for Africa because the youngest, healthiest, and best workers were taken.

B. Reviewing Key Terms

Directions: Write the definition for each key term below.

11. encomienda

____

12. conquistador

____

CHAPTER 7
Changes in the Western World

Limits on Monarchs

A. As You Read

Directions: As you read Section 1, fill in the table below with information about the monarchy in England.

The Monarchy in England

Henry VIII	1. 2.
Elizabeth I	3. 4.
Conflicts Between Monarchy and Parliament	5. 6.
Constitutional Monarchy	7. 8.

B. Reviewing Key Terms

Directions: For each definition below, write the correct key term in the blank provided.

9. a war for power among groups within a single country ______________________

10. an overthrow of a government or a sudden change in the way people think

    ____

11. a summary of all the rights held by a people under their government ______________________

12. a government in which the monarch's power is limited by a set of laws

    ____

The Enlightenment

A. As You Read

Directions: As you read Section 2, answer the following questions on a separate sheet of paper.

1. What question did Galileo answer falsely to the Catholic Church court? Why did he do this?

2. To what source can many of the new ideas of the Enlightenment be traced?

3. What was more important to Galileo and other scientists than traditional beliefs?

4. What things did John Locke question? What did he believe about nature?

5. What are two conclusions that Locke drew about governments?

6. How did people find out about the ideas of Locke and other thinkers of his day?

7. Why were the colonists in North America angry at the British?

8. What did Thomas Jefferson say in the Declaration of Independence about the right of governments to rule?

B. Reviewing Key Terms

Directions: In the blanks provided, write the definitions for the following key terms.

9. Enlightenment

____

10. scientific method

____

____

11. natural law

____

12. colony

____

The Industrial Revolution

A. As You Read

Directions: As you read Section 3, complete the statements below.

1. The _____________________ changed the ways in which people today work, shop, and spend their free time.

2. Before the Industrial Revolution, only the very _____________________ had more than one change of clothes.

3. One worker using a _____________________ could do the work of eight people using spinning wheels.

4. Two ways in which early machines were supplied with power were by

   _____________________ and _____________________ .

5. The Industrial Revolution created new jobs and allowed more people to move into the

   _____________________ of society.

6. Many farmers and poor people's lives became _____________________ during the Industrial Revolution.

7. As more and more goods were made in factories, people had to move to

   _____________________ to earn a living.

8. For many factory workers, including children, life was nothing but endless

   _____________________ .

9. The working and living conditions were so bad for most factory workers that even minor

   diseases could be _____________________ .

B. Reviewing Key Terms

Directions: Complete each sentence by writing the correct term in the blank provided.

10. During the _____________________ , many workers who had worked at home began to work in factories.

11. The _____________________ industry was one of the first to move into factories.

12. The working conditions in British factories were so terrible that workers organized

    _____________________ to fight for decent wages and working conditions.

GUIDED READING AND REVIEW

Revolution and Imperialism

CHAPTER 7
Changes in the Western World

A. As You Read

Directions: As you read Section 4, fill in the table below with information about revolution and imperialism. Under each main idea, write two supporting details.

Main Idea A
The French Revolution grew out of the mistreatment of the people and led to a time of terror.

1. ____

2. ____

Main Idea B
Napoleon Bonaparte led France to victory and brought about many reforms.

3. ____

4. ____

Main Idea C
As European nations became more powerful, they began to expand their power in other lands.

5. ____

6. ____

B. Reviewing Key Terms

Directions: Complete each sentence by writing the correct term in the blank provided.

7. During the _______________________ in France, 70 to 80 people were killed each day.

8. The _______________________ was a rewritten form of the laws of France that made them clear and easy to understand.

9. As nations became more powerful, people began to gain an increased sense of _______________________ , or pride in their country.

10. Many European countries created empires of colonies through a policy of _______________________ .

World Wars and Revolution

A. As You Read

Directions: As you read Section 1, fill in the table below with information about world wars and revolutions during the 1900s. Write several facts for each topic.

World Wars and Revolution

Russian Revolution	**1.**
Nationalism	**2.**
World War I	**3.**
World War II	**4.**

B. Reviewing Key Terms

Directions: On a separate sheet of paper, write the definition for each key term.

5. czar

6. serf

7. communism

8. alliance

9. armistice

10. genocide

11. Holocaust

12. atomic bomb

Breaking Colonial Ties

A. As You Read

Directions: As you read Section 2, answer the following questions in the space provided.

1. What happened to other African nations after the Gold Coast won its independence?

____

2. What are two reasons that people from colonized areas wanted to end European rule?

____

____

3. After World War II, what did colonies that had fought on Britain's side want?

____

4. How many African countries had gained their independence by 1990?

____

5. What happened to India after it won its independence from Britain in 1947?

____

6. What are some of the challenges faced by newly independent nations?

____

____

7. How did racism affect life in South Africa for many years?

____

8. What happened in South Africa in 1994?

____

B. Reviewing Key Terms

Directions: Complete each sentence by writing the correct term in the blank provided.

9. Gandhi used ___________________ to win independence for India.

10. For many years, South African laws promoted ___________________ among the people.

11. Many former colonies have few industries and are among the world's

___________________ .

12. Most countries that used to have colonies are ___________________ and have many industries.

CHAPTER 8
**A Century
of Turmoil**

Our Shrinking Globe

A. As You Read

Directions: As you read Section 3, complete the statements below.

 1. The two superpowers that led the capitalist and communist worlds after World War II

   were the ____________________ and the ____________________ .

 2. During the Cold War, the superpowers built enough ____________________ to destroy
   the world.

 3. Two "hot" wars that broke out during the Cold War took place in ____________________

   and ____________________ .

 4. The Cold War ended when ____________________ collapsed in Eastern Europe and the
   Soviet Union.

 5. Controlling ____________________ has become one of the major challenges of today's
   world.

B. Reviewing Key Terms

Directions: For each definition below, write the correct key term in the blank
provided.

 6. the rejoining of East and West Germany as one nation in 1989 ____________________

 7. a country in which people can own businesses and factories and can compete to make

   a profit ____________________

 8. the period between 1945 and 1991 when there was distrust, suspicion, and increased risk

   of war between capitalist and communist countries ____________________

 9. the attempt by the United States and the Soviet Union to build the most nuclear weapons

   ____

10. dependent upon one another ____________________